W9-CJL-386

WILD AMERICA

DEER

By Lee Jacobs

BLACKBIRCH®
PRESS

THOMSON

GALE

San Diego • Detroit • New York • San Francisco • Cleveland • New Haven, Conn. • Waterville, Maine • London • Munich

THOMSON

GALE

For Liza

For more information, contact
The Gale Group, Inc.
27500 Drake Rd.
Farmington Hills, MI 48331-3535
Or you can visit our Internet site at http://www.gale.com

Photo Credits: Cover, back cover, pages 4, 7, 8, 11, 21, 22 © PhotoDisc; pages 3, 16, 17 © Tom and Pat Leeson Nature Wildlife Photography; pages 5, 6, 10, 12, 13, 14, 15, 17, 18, 19 © Corel; pages 9, 20 © Digital Stock; page 23 © Art Today

LIBRARY OF CONGRESS CATALOGING-IN-PUBLICATION DATA

Jacobs, Lee.
  Deer / by Lee Jacobs.
      p. cm. — (Wild America)
Includes bibliographical references.
Summary: Examines the deer's environment, anatomy, social life, food, mating habits, and relationship with humans.
  ISBN 1-56711-643-4 (hardback : alk. paper)
  1. Deer—Juvenile literature. [1. Deer.] I. Title. II. Series.
  QL737.U55 J342 2003
  599.65—dc21
                                                                2002002473

Printed in China
10 9 8 7 6 5 4 3 2 1

Contents

Introduction 4

The Deer's Environment 6

The Deer Body 8

Social Life 12

Finding Food 14

The Mating Game 18

Fawns 20

Deer and Humans 22

Glossary 24

Further Reading 24

Index 24

Introduction

Deer are the largest wild animals that make their homes near humans. People who live near North American woods and swamplands are likely to have deer as neighbors.

Deer are mammals that belong to the Cervidae family. There are five major species in North America—white-tailed deer, blacktail or mule deer, moose, caribou, and elk.

Deer often live in swamplands and woods.

Blacktail deer live in the western part of the United States. White-tailed deer are found throughout the United States, Mexico, and Canada. This is the kind of deer that has the most contact with people. There are more than 30 million white-tailed deer in North America today.

Deer are the largest wild animals that live near humans

The Deer's Environment

Deer like to live in areas that have both open meadows and woodlands. They do not build homes or nests as many other animals do. When it is time to sleep, they simply lie down where they are. It may be in the snow, in tall grass, or on the soft leaves or needles beneath a tree. This is their bed for the night.

Deer have large home ranges because they spend most of their time roaming around. The range must provide food, water, and safe places to hide.

Deer lie down where they are when they are ready to sleep.

Deer use scent markings to tell other deer to stay out of their territory. Deer mark their ranges with a scent that comes from a gland in front of each eye.

It is easy to tell if there are deer in an area. Tree bark that looks scraped is a sign that deer have passed by. Large, slightly sunken areas underneath a tree may be places where deer have rested. If plants are missing many of their buds, deer have probably fed on them.

Deer spend most of their time roamng and grazing.

The Deer Body

A deer's body is slim. Its coat is usually a reddish tan color during the warmer seasons. In winter, the fur becomes a dull gray. White-tailed deer get their name from the white fur on the undersides of their tails. The deer's shape and color help it blend in very well with its woodland habitat. Standing very still, this large animal becomes almost invisible to predators in the forest.

The average deer is about 3.5 feet (1 m) tall and weighs 120 pounds (54 kg). Some large males can weigh up to 400 pounds (182 kg). Most deer are about 6 feet (2 m) long.

Deer have slim bodies and long, thin legs.

Deer have long, thin legs that are strong and powerful. They can leap 10 feet (3 m) in the air and run more than 35 miles (56 km) per hour. They can also switch directions quickly and constantly. Such speed and agility helps them escape predators. If a predator gets too close, a deer can quickly zigzag out of the way.

A deer's hoof has two big, horn-covered toes in front. These hooves provide a steady footing in slippery spots. Deer can also use their hooves to dig into deep snow and find grass, or to kick an enemy. At the back of each hoof are two small toes called dewclaws.

A deer can leap and zigzag to escape predators.

Deer have excellent hearing and eyesight. Their large ears help them hear sounds from a great distance. They can move one ear at a time, so deer can hear sounds coming from two different directions. Sharp vision allows deer to notice even the tiniest movement in their surroundings. On its nose, a deer has soft black skin that stays moist. Scent particles floating in the air stick to the wet nose. This gives the deer a keen sense of smell. These sharp senses help deer to survive by quickly alerting them to danger.

Deer have a special kind of nose that gives them a keen sense of smell.

Not all deer have antlers. Only males (bucks) of the Cervidae family develop antlers. Antlers are made of solid bone and have a soft, fuzzy outer covering called velvet. Tiny blood vessels run through the velvet. They supply the antlers with the blood they need to grow. The antlers of a one-year-old buck usually have just a single tip, or point. Each year, a buck grows a new set of antlers. As a deer ages, each new set of antlers grows larger. The antlers start to have branches, and each branch has several points.

Antlers begin to grow in the spring. By the end of the summer or beginning of the fall, their growth is complete. At this point, the velvet begins to dry and fall off. A deer will rub its antlers against a tree to scrape off the peeling pieces of velvet. (He may also do this to mark his territory by leaving his scent.) Each winter, antlers are shed (dropped off) one by one. Small animals, such as squirrels and mice, nibble on fallen antlers for nourishment.

Antlers have a soft, fuzzy covering.

Social Life

Bucks often keep to themselves, but they may also form small herds (groups) apart from the females. Female deer are called does. Does only pair up with bucks during mating season. For most of the year, does and their babies live apart from the bucks.

Does and their young often live and feed together in small herds. Each herd has a lead doe. Her job is to be on the lookout for danger. She alerts the group whenever her eyes, ears, or nose detect trouble. To warn her herd, the lead doe stomps one hoof and snorts loudly.

Top: Deer flash the white undersides of their tails to signal danger.
Bottom: Deer are constantly on the lookout for danger.

The other does then lift their tails and flash their white undersides to signal danger. This is called "tail-flagging." Besides alerting the herd to danger, tail-flagging helps fawns (baby deer) see and follow their mothers as they run away from the threat. (Bucks also display their white tails as a danger signal.)

Deer communicate by both sound and smell. In addition to snorts, they make many other noises. Special glands in several areas of their bodies produce different scents. These scents are used to mark territory, to show that a buck is dominant (the leader), and to tell males that a doe is ready to mate.

Top: Bucks may live alone or in a small herd.
Bottom: Female deer and their young live together in small herds.

13

Finding Food

Deer are herbivores, which means they only eat plants. When there is plenty of food, white-tailed deer will eat about 10 to 12 pounds (4.5 to 5 kg) of food a day. Deer eat all kinds of plant foods. As they walk through the forest, deer nibble on twigs, shoots, buds, leaves, stems, and bark. They also love nuts and fruit, such as acorns, berries, and apples. Deer will eat lightly throughout the day, but they mostly feed at twilight.

Deer can eat up to 12 pounds (5 kg) of plant foods a day.

In winter, when finding food is difficult, deer may only eat a few pounds of food a day. They will dig into the snow to uncover any remaining grass or needles from evergreen trees. During the cold winter months, deer will eat more tree bark and tall brush. Some deer die of starvation or cold during unusually long or harsh winters.

Deer have a variety of teeth that help them eat many kinds of plants. They use their front lower teeth to pull off grass and leaves. Their back lower teeth grind and mash rough plant materials.

In winter, deer may dig under snow to find food.

Deer do not have front teeth in their upper jaw. Instead, there is a pad that helps them grip the food in their mouth while they chew.

Deer have four-chambered stomachs. When they swallow food, it is stored in the first stomach compartment, the rumen. Later, the deer brings the partially chewed food up from the rumen and chews it again. The food that is brought up from the rumen is called the cud.

Deer use their front teeth to snip off leaves.

After the deer swallows the cud, it is digested in the other three stomach chambers. This special stomach helps deer survive. With it, they can quickly swallow a large amount of food, then wait until they are safely hidden in the forest to chew their cud.

Deer eat twigs, bark, buds, and leaves.

The Mating Game

The rut, or mating season, for deer begins in late August and lasts until January. Both males and females become able to mate before they are 2 years old. Does only mate for a period of 1 to 2 days each month during mating season.

A buck will mate with several does during the rut. Bucks spend less time eating and more time looking for mates during breeding season. They become more aggressive and will often challenge other bucks for mating rights to a doe.

Bucks and does only stay together for a short time during mating season.

Bucks with the largest, strongest antlers usually win the fight over a female.

When two bucks fight for a doe, they lock antlers and shove each other back and forth. This is called "sparring." The two bucks fight until one of them either gives up or runs away. The buck with the largest, strongest antlers usually wins. Once a doe is pregnant, it will be between 190 and 210 days before her fawn is born.

Fawns

Does give birth once a year, in the spring or early summer. First-time mothers usually have one fawn. After that, they generally have two. Fawns weigh between 4 and 6 pounds (2 to 3 kg) at birth. Just after a baby is born, a doe will lick her fawn all over its body. This cleans and dries the young animal. It also helps to improve the fawn's blood circulation.

The scent of the birth site often attracts predators. To protect her babies, a doe will gently nudge the fawns, encouraging them to stand up as soon as they are born. The mother then leads her fawns away from the birth site. Fawns will nurse for about 8 months. At about 2 months, they will begin to eat plants.

A baby deer, or fawn, nurses until it is about eight months old.

Fawns are born with a variety of natural defenses that help protect them from predators.

A fawn's hair is marked with white spots until it is a few months old. When it is a newborn, a fawn stays nestled in its bed. The spots help the deer blend into the mix of sun and shadows in the forest, which makes it hard for enemies to see it. Fawns do not have any body odor for the first few weeks. This makes it difficult for a predator to find a fawn by smell. Because the doe's scent could attract predators, she watches her babies from a safe distance. Does may also defend their fawns by placing themselves between a predator and their young. They may also run away from the fawn to distract an enemy.

As fawns get older, they learn to act like adults. They fight playfully with one another, chase each other, run, and learn how to find food. A fawn stays with its mother for about a year before going off on its own.

Fawns have spotted fur that helps them blend in with their surroundings.

Deer and Humans

Deer have many natural enemies, including bears, wolves, coyotes, and mountain lions. Humans also hunt deer. Some people hunt them for their meat, which is called venison. People use deerskin to make gloves and shoes. Deer hunting is also a popular sport in many parts of America.

As human populations grow, there is less wild area for deer.

In some areas, deer hunting is necessary to control the population. If there are too many deer, especially in areas where they compete for territory with humans, many deer will die from lack of food. Thousands of deer are also killed each year by cars.

Deer often have to live near people. It is not unusual to see deer in the backyards of many homes in America.

In fact, one of the safer environments for deer is in suburbs. Hunting is not allowed in these areas and animals that prey on deer do not normally live there. Some people welcome the deer and leave food out for them. Other people become annoyed when deer take food from their gardens or fruit orchards.

As towns and cities grow, the wild places where deer live continue to disappear. That means that deer and people will most likely remain neighbors for a long time to come.

Above: Some deer become completely unafraid of humans.
Below: Cars kill thousands of deer each year.

Glossary

buck a male deer

cud partially chewed food brought up from the rumen

dewclaws the small toes on the back of a deer hoof

doe a female deer

dominant the leader of a group; the most powerful member of a group

fawn a baby deer

herbivore an animal that eats plants

herd a group of deer

predator an animal that hunts another animal for food

rumen the first compartment of a four-chambered stomach

ruminant an animal that chews its cud

rut the mating season

sparring fighting; competing by locking antlers

suburb a smaller town or community located just outside a big city

velvet the fuzzy outer covering of antlers

venison deer meat

Further Reading

Books

Arnosky, Jim. *All About Deer* (All About). New York: Scholastic, 1999.

Berendes, Mary. *Deer* (Naturebooks). Chanhassen, MN: Child's World, 1999.

Evert, Laura. *Whitetail Deer* (Our Wild World). Minnetonka, MN: Creative Publishing International, 2000.

Johnson, Jinny. *Deer* (Busy Baby Animals). Milwaukee, WI: Gareth Stevens, 2001.

Simon, Serge. *The Deer* (Animal Close-ups). Watertown, MA: Charlesbridge, 1993.

Index

Bucks,
  antlers, 11
  group of, 12
  mating rights, 18-19

Cervidae family, 4, 11
Cud, 16

Deer,
  antlers, 11
  blacktailed, 5
  body, 8
  coat, 8
  communication, 13
  ears, 10

eyesight, 10
hooves, 9
legs, 9
teeth, 15, 16
white-tailed, 5, 8, 14
Does,
  giving birth, 20
  group of, 12
  mating, 18
  raising young, 21

Fawns,
  birth of, 20
  body of, 21
  protection of, 13, 21

Food, 14, 15

Herds, 12
Home range, 6
Hunting, 22-23

Mating, 18

Scent marking, 7
Sparring, 19

Tail flagging, 13